curries

curries

fragrant & spicy dishes

This edition published in 2010
LOVE FOOD is an imprint of Parragon Books Ltd

Parragon
Queen Street House
4 Queen Street
Bath BA1 1HE, UK

Copyright © Parragon Books Ltd 2005

LOVE FOOD and the accompanying heart device is a registered trademark of Parragon
Books Ltd in Australia, the UK, US, and the EU.

ISBN: 978-1-4454-0699-2

Printed in China

Produced by the Bridgewater Book Company Ltd
Design concept by Fiona Roberts

Notes for the Reader
This book uses imperial, metric, and US cup measurements. Follow the same units of
measurement throughout; do not mix imperial and metric. All spoon measurements are
level: teaspoons are assumed to be 5 ml, and tablespoons are assumed to be 15 ml. Unless
otherwise stated, milk is assumed to be whole, eggs and individual vegetables such as
potatoes are medium, and pepper is freshly ground black pepper.

The times given are an approximate guide only. Preparation times differ according to the
techniques used by different people and the cooking times may also vary from those given
as a result of the type of oven used. Optional ingredients, variations or serving suggestions
have not been included in the calculations.

Recipes using raw or very lightly cooked eggs should be avoided by infants, the elderly,
pregnant women, convalescents, and anyone with a chronic condition. Pregnant and
breastfeeding women are advised to avoid eating peanuts and peanut products. Sufferers
from nut allergies should be aware that some of the ready-prepared ingredients used in the
recipes in this book may contain nuts. Always check the packaging before use.

Vegetarians should be aware that some of the ready-prepared ingredients used in the
recipes in this book may contain animal products. Always check the packaging before use.

Introduction

CURRY DESCRIBES A STYLE OF COOKING USING A SPICED AND SEASONED GRAVY. THE WORD "CURRY" HAS HUMBLE ROOTS, AS IT IS THE TAMIL WORD FOR SAUCE. IT WAS THE BRITISH IN INDIA DURING THE 18TH CENTURY WHO ADOPTED IT, MODIFIED IT, AND PLACED IT ON ITS ELEVATED PATH, AND IT IS NOW A HUGELY POPULAR INTERNATIONAL DISH. INDIA IS THE MAIN HOME OF CURRY, FOLLOWED BY PAKISTAN, AFGHANISTAN, AND THAILAND, BUT CURRY IS EATEN WORLDWIDE. CURRIES VARY ENORMOUSLY ACCORDING TO REGION, RELIGION, CUSTOMS, AND LOCAL INGREDIENTS, BUT ALL ARE SAVORY AND SPICED. THEY CAN BE FIERY OR GENTLE DEPENDING ON THE CHILIES AND SEASONINGS USED. INDIAN CURRIES ARE MADE WITH A MIXTURE OF SPICES KNOWN AS MASALA. THAI CURRIES ARE MADE USING A PASTE OF CHILIES, HERBS, VEGETABLES, AND SPICES. THE BASIC THAI CURRY PASTE RECIPES ARE GIVEN OPPOSITE AND ARE USED IN THE RECIPES IN THE BOOK.

Basic recipes

THAI YELLOW CURRY PASTE

3 small fresh orange or yellow chilies,
    coarsely chopped
3 large garlic cloves, coarsely chopped
4 shallots, coarsely chopped
3 tsp ground turmeric
1 tsp salt
12–15 black peppercorns
1 lemon grass stalk (white part only),
    coarsely chopped
1-inch/2.5-cm piece fresh gingerroot, chopped

• Put all the ingredients in a food processor or
blender and process to a thick paste, scraping
down the sides as necessary.

THAI RED CURRY PASTE

1 tbsp coriander seeds
1 tbsp cumin seeds
2 tsp shrimp paste
12 dried or fresh red chilies, chopped
2 shallots, chopped
8 garlic cloves, chopped
1-inch/2.5-cm piece fresh galangal,
    chopped
2 lemon grass stalks (white part only),
    chopped
4 kaffir lime leaves, chopped
2 tbsp chopped fresh cilantro root
grated rind of 1 lime
1 tsp black peppercorns

• Dry-fry the coriander and cumin seeds in a
skillet, stirring constantly, for 2–3 minutes
until browned. Remove from the heat and
grind to a powder using a pestle and mortar.
Wrap the shrimp paste in a piece of foil and
broil or dry-fry in a skillet for 2–3 minutes,
turning once or twice. Put the ground spices,
shrimp paste, and chilies in a food processor
or blender and process until finely chopped.
Add the remaining ingredients and process
again to a smooth paste, scraping down the
sides as necessary.

THAI GREEN CURRY PASTE

• Follow the instructions for Red Curry
Paste, but replace the chilies with 15 fresh
green Thai chilies, use only 6 garlic cloves,
increase the number of kaffir lime leaves to 6,
and add 1 teaspoon of salt with the pepper.

MUSSAMAN CURRY PASTE

4 large dried red chilies, stalks removed
2 tsp shrimp paste
3 shallots, finely chopped
3 garlic cloves, finely chopped
1-inch/2.5-cm piece fresh galangal, finely
    chopped
2 lemon grass stalks (white part only),
    finely chopped
2 cloves
1 tbsp coriander seeds
1 tbsp cumin seeds
seeds from 3 green cardamom pods
1 tsp black peppercorns
1 tsp salt

• Place the chilies in a bowl, cover with hot
water, and set aside to soak for 30–45
minutes. Wrap the shrimp paste in foil and
broil or dry-fry in a skillet for 2–3 minutes,
turning once or twice. Remove from the
broiler or skillet. Dry-fry the shallots, garlic,
galangal, lemon grass, cloves, and coriander,
cumin, and cardamom seeds over low heat,
stirring frequently, for 3–4 minutes until
lightly browned. Transfer to a food processor
and process until finely ground. Add the
chilies and their soaking water, peppercorns,
and salt, and process again. Add the shrimp
paste and process again to a smooth paste,
scraping down the sides as necessary.

GARLIC AND GINGER PASTE

• Blend together equal quantities of garlic and
fresh gingerroot. Store in a sealed jar in the
refrigerator for up to 3 weeks, or in the freezer
for up to 1 month.

India has a population of nearly a billion people, with probably the largest and most diverse mixture of races and religions in the world. The mix of Buddhists, Christians, Hindus, Jains, Muslims, and Parsis, along with the racial structure and varied geographical conditions, play a large part in the enormous variety of India's cuisines.

To Hindus, the cow is considered sacred, so they do not eat beef or veal, and some eat no meat at all. Muslims don't eat pork, but Indian Christians eat both pork and beef, as featured in the traditional recipes, Pork Vindaloo and Beef Madras. Pork is also the first choice in Thai and Burmese curries. The number one choice for Indian curries is lamb, as sheep are bred in the cooler, northern areas of India. Rogan Josh, for example, is a traditional favorite. Mutton and goat are also popular meats.

MEAT AND POULTRY PERFECTION

Chicken, too, is an ideal meat for using in curries, as it cooks quickly and is tender and succulent. The skin should always be removed prior to cooking to enable the spices to penetrate the chicken flesh better. Duck is also popular in Thai curries, and boneless duck breasts could be substituted for any of the chicken recipes in this chapter. Another practical point is that many meat curries benefit from being made in advance, cooled, chilled, and then thoroughly reheated, as this allows the spices to come together and the flavor of the dish to mature. What are you waiting for?

SERVES 4–6

2 tbsp ghee or vegetable or peanut oil

1 large onion, chopped

2 garlic cloves, crushed

2 large red bell peppers, seeded and chopped

1 lb 5 oz/600 g sirloin steak, thinly sliced

fresh cilantro sprigs, to garnish

BALTI SAUCE

2 tbsp ghee or vegetable or peanut oil

2 large onions, chopped

1 tbsp Garlic and Ginger Paste

14 oz/400 g canned chopped tomatoes

1 tsp ground paprika

½ tsp ground turmeric

½ tsp ground cumin

½ tsp ground coriander

¼ tsp chili powder

¼ tsp ground cardamom

1 bay leaf

salt and pepper

Balti Beef

The Balti Sauce can be be made in advance and refrigerated for several days, making this recipe perfect for a quick-cooking midweek meal.

• To make the Balti Sauce, melt the ghee in a karahi, wok, or large skillet over medium-high heat. Add the onions and Garlic and Ginger Paste and stir-fry for 5 minutes until the onions are golden brown. Stir in the tomatoes with their juices, then add the paprika, turmeric, cumin, coriander, chili powder, cardamom, bay leaf, and salt and pepper to taste. Bring the mixture to a boil, stirring constantly, then reduce the heat and let simmer for 20 minutes, stirring occasionally.

• Let the sauce cool slightly, then remove the bay leaf and pour the mixture into a food processor or blender. Whiz to a smooth sauce.

• Wipe out the karahi, wok, or skillet and return it to medium-high heat. Add the ghee and melt. Add the onion and garlic and stir-fry for 5–8 minutes until golden brown. Add the red bell peppers and continue stir-frying for 2 minutes.

• Stir in the beef and continue stir-frying for 2 minutes until it starts to turn brown. Add the Balti Sauce and bring to a boil. Reduce the heat and simmer for 5 minutes, or until the sauce slightly reduces again and the bell pepper is tender. Adjust the seasoning, if necessary, and garnish with cilantro sprigs. Serve in a karahi, if liked.

SERVES 4–6

1 tbsp ground coriander

1 tbsp ground cumin

3 tbsp Mussaman Curry Paste

2/3 cup water

2¾ oz/75 g creamed coconut

1 lb/450 g beef fillet, cut into strips

1¾ cups canned coconut milk

1/3 cup unsalted peanuts, finely
    chopped

2 tbsp Thai fish sauce

1 tsp palm sugar or brown sugar

4 kaffir lime leaves

fresh cilantro sprigs, to garnish

Coconut Beef Curry

The kaffir lime leaves add a citrus flavor to this Thai curry, but if you are unable to buy them, lime rind makes an adequate substitute. When you do find kaffir lime leaves, buy lots, as they freeze well.

• Combine the coriander, cumin, and Mussaman Curry Paste in a bowl. Pour the water into a pan, add the creamed coconut, and heat until it has dissolved. Add the curry paste mixture and simmer for 1 minute.

• Add the beef and simmer for 6–8 minutes, then add the coconut milk, peanuts, fish sauce, and sugar. Simmer gently for 15–20 minutes, or until the meat is tender. Add the lime leaves and simmer for 1–2 minutes. Transfer to bowls and garnish with cilantro sprigs. Serve hot.

SERVES 4–6

1–2 dried red chilies

2 tsp ground coriander

2 tsp ground turmeric

1 tsp black mustard seeds

½ tsp ground ginger

¼ tsp ground pepper

5 oz/140 g creamed coconut,
    grated and dissolved in
    1¼ cups boiling water

4 tbsp ghee or vegetable or peanut oil

2 onions, chopped

3 large garlic cloves, chopped

1 lb 9 oz/700 g lean chuck steak,
    trimmed and cut into 2-inch/5-cm
    cubes

generous 1 cup beef stock

1 tbsp lemon juice

salt

fresh cilantro sprigs, to garnish

Beef Madras

The dish takes on a different character, but is equally flavorsome, if you omit the chilies altogether and garnish the dish with toasted coconut flakes just before serving.

• Depending on how hot you want this dish to be, chop the chilies with or without any seeds. (The more seeds you include, the hotter the dish will be.) Put the chopped chili and any seeds in a small bowl with the coriander, turmeric, mustard seeds, ginger, and pepper and stir in a little of the coconut mixture to make a thin paste.

• Melt the ghee in a flameproof casserole or large skillet with a tight-fitting lid over medium-high heat. Add the onions and garlic and cook for 5–8 minutes, stirring frequently, until the onions are golden brown. Add the spice paste and stir-fry for 2 minutes, or until you can smell the aromas.

• Add the beef and stock and bring to a boil. Reduce the heat to its lowest level, cover, and simmer for 90 minutes, or until the beef is tender. Check occasionally that the meat isn't catching on the bottom of the pan and stir in a little extra water or stock, if necessary.

• Uncover the pan and stir in the remaining coconut mixture with the lemon juice and salt to taste. Bring to a boil, stirring, then reduce the heat and simmer, still uncovered, until the sauce reduces slightly. Garnish with cilantro sprigs and serve.

SERVES 4–6

1 tbsp vegetable or peanut oil

1 lb/450 g boneless rump roast,
  cut into cubes

2 tbsp Mussaman Curry Paste

2 large onions, cut into wedges

2 large potatoes, cut into chunks

1¾ cups canned coconut milk

⅔ cup water

2 green cardamom pods

2 tbsp tamarind paste

2 tsp palm sugar or brown sugar

½ cup unsalted peanuts, toasted
  or dry-fried

1 fresh red chili, thinly sliced

Mussaman Curry

Mussaman means "Muslim." This Thai Mussaman curry originated in the south, where spices brought by Indian traders gradually made their way into Thai cooking. Based on chilies, it also contains coriander, cumin, and lemon grass.

• Heat the oil in a skillet or wok. Add the meat, in batches, and cook until browned all over. Remove with a slotted spoon and reserve.

• Add the Mussaman Curry Paste to the pan and stir-fry for 1–2 minutes. Add the onions and potatoes and stir-fry for 4–5 minutes until golden brown. Remove with a slotted spoon and reserve.

• Pour the coconut milk into the pan with the water and bring to a boil. Reduce the heat and let simmer for 8–10 minutes.

• Return the meat and cooked vegetables to the pan. Add the cardamom pods, tamarind paste, and sugar and simmer for 15–20 minutes, or until the meat is tender. Stir in the peanuts and chili and serve hot.

SERVES 4–6

2 tbsp ghee or vegetable oil

1 onion, chopped

1 cinnamon stick

4 green cardamom pods, lightly
    crushed

1 curry leaf

4 cloves

2 tsp Garlic and Ginger Paste

1 lb/450 g ground lamb

2 tsp ground coriander

2 tsp ground cumin

1 tsp chili powder

2/3 cup plain yogurt

1 tbsp ground fenugreek

salt

coarsely shredded fresh cilantro,
    to garnish

Lamb Keema

In India, this dish would be flavored with fresh fenugreek leaves, known as methi. If available, use 1 bunch of fresh leaves. Always remove and discard the bitter stems.

• Melt the ghee in a karahi, wok, or large, heavy-bottom pan. Add the onion and cook over low heat, stirring occasionally, for 5 minutes, or until softened.

• Add the cinnamon stick, cardamom pods, curry leaf, and cloves and cook, stirring constantly, for 1 minute, then add the Garlic and Ginger Paste and cook, stirring constantly, for an additional 1 minute.

• Add the ground lamb and sprinkle over the coriander, cumin, and chili powder. Cook for 5 minutes, or until the lamb is lightly browned, stirring and breaking up the meat with a wooden spoon.

• Stir in the yogurt and fenugreek and season to taste with salt. Cover and cook over low heat for 20–30 minutes, or until the lamb is tender and the liquid has been absorbed. Ladle into a warmed serving dish and discard the curry leaf. Garnish with coarsely shredded cilantro and serve immediately.

SERVES 4–6

1 lb 9 oz/700 g boneless leg of lamb, trimmed and cut into 2-inch/5-cm cubes

2 tomatoes, seeded and chopped

1 onion, chopped

2 tbsp ghee or vegetable or peanut oil

1½ tbsp Garlic and Ginger Paste

2 tbsp tomato paste

2 bay leaves

1 tbsp ground coriander

¼–1 tsp chili powder, ideally Kashmiri chili powder

½ tsp ground turmeric

1 tsp salt

½ tsp garam masala

fresh bay leaves, to garnish (optional)

MARINADE

1½ cups plain yogurt

½ tsp ground asafetida, dissolved in 2 tbsp water

Rogan Josh

For an authentic flavor, search out the bright-red Kashmiri chili powder sold at Indian markets.

• To make the marinade, put the yogurt in a large bowl and stir in the asafetida. Add the lamb and use your hands to rub in all the marinade, then cover and let marinate in a cool place for 30 minutes.

• Meanwhile, put the tomatoes and onion in a food processor or blender and whiz until blended. Melt the ghee in a flameproof casserole or large skillet with a tight-fitting lid. Add the Garlic and Ginger Paste and stir-fry until you can smell cooked garlic.

• Stir in the tomato mixture, tomato paste, bay leaves, coriander, chili powder, and turmeric. Reduce the heat to low and simmer, stirring occasionally, for 5–8 minutes.

• Add the lamb with any leftover marinade and the salt and cook, stirring, for 2 minutes. Cover, reduce the heat to low, and simmer, stirring occasionally, for 30 minutes. The lamb should give off enough moisture to prevent it catching on the bottom of the pan, but if the sauce looks too dry, stir in a little water.

• Sprinkle the lamb with the garam masala, re-cover the pan, and continue simmering for an additional 15–20 minutes, or until the lamb is tender. Adjust the seasoning, if necessary. Garnish the curry with bay leaves, if liked, and serve.

SERVES 4–6

1 lb 9 oz/700 g boneless shoulder
of lamb
1 tbsp Garlic and Ginger Paste
5 green cardamom pods
1 cup yellow lentils
3½ oz/100 g peeled, seeded, and
chopped pumpkin
1 carrot, thinly sliced

1 fresh green chili, seeded and
chopped
1 tsp ground fenugreek
generous 2 cups water
1 large onion, thinly sliced
2 tbsp ghee or vegetable or peanut oil
2 garlic cloves, crushed
salt
chopped fresh cilantro, to garnish

DHANSAK MASALA
1 tsp garam masala
½ tsp ground coriander
½ tsp ground cumin
½ tsp chili powder
½ tsp ground turmeric
¼ tsp ground cardamom
¼ tsp ground cloves

Lamb Dhansak

If you don't have time
to make the masala,
look in Indian markets for
packages of ready-made
dhansak masala. Add
1 tablespoon to the onions
and continue with the
recipe as above.

• Trim and cut the lamb into 2-inch/5-cm cubes. Put the lamb and 1 teaspoon salt in a large pan with enough water to cover and bring to a boil. Reduce the heat and simmer, skimming the surface as necessary, until no more foam rises. Stir in the Garlic and Ginger Paste and cardamom pods and continue simmering for a total of 30 minutes.

• Meanwhile, put the lentils, pumpkin, carrot, chili, and fenugreek in a large, heavy-bottom pan and pour over the water. Bring to a boil, stirring occasionally, then reduce the heat and simmer for 20–30 minutes until the lentils and carrot are very tender. Stir in a little extra water if the lentils look as though they will catch on the bottom of the pan.

• Let the lentil mixture cool slightly, then pour it into a food processor or blender and whiz until a thick, smooth sauce forms.

• While the lamb and lentils are cooking, put the onion in a bowl, sprinkle with 1 teaspoon salt, and let stand for about 5 minutes to extract the moisture. Use your hands to squeeze out any excess.

• Melt the ghee in a flameproof casserole or large skillet with a tight-fitting lid over high heat. Add the onion and cook, stirring constantly, for 2 minutes. Remove one-third of the onion and continue cooking the rest for an additional 1–2 minutes until golden brown. Use a slotted spoon to remove them immediately from the pan, as they will continue to darken as they cool.

• Return the smaller quantity of onion to the pan with the garlic. Stir in all the Dhansak Masala ingredients and cook for 2 minutes, stirring constantly. Add the cooked lamb and stir for an additional 2 minutes. Add the lentil sauce and simmer over medium heat to warm through, stirring and adding a little extra water, if needed. Adjust the seasoning, if necessary. Sprinkle with the dark onion and cilantro and serve.

SERVES 4–6

1 lb 5 oz/600 g boneless lamb shoulder or leg

2 tbsp Garlic and Ginger Paste

4 tbsp ghee or vegetable or peanut oil

3 large onions, chopped

1 fresh green chili, seeded and chopped (optional)

2 green cardamom pods, lightly crushed

1 cinnamon stick, broken in half

2 tsp ground coriander

1 tsp ground cumin

1 tsp ground turmeric

generous 1 cup water

2/3 cup heavy cream

4 tbsp ground almonds

1½ tsp salt

1 tsp garam masala

TO GARNISH

paprika

toasted slivered almonds

Lamb Pasanda

A legacy from the glorious days of the Moghul courts, when Indian cooking reached a refined peak, this rich, creamy dish gets its name from the word "pasanda," which means small pieces of boneless meat, in this case tender lamb, flattened as thinly as possible.

• Cut the meat into thin slices, then place the slices between plastic wrap and bash with a rolling pin or meat mallet to make them even thinner. Put the lamb slices in a bowl, add the Garlic and Ginger Paste, and use your hands to rub the paste into the lamb. Cover and let marinate in a cool place for 2 hours.

• Melt the ghee in a flameproof casserole or large skillet with a tight-fitting lid over medium-high heat. Add the onion and chili, if using, and cook, stirring frequently, for 5–8 minutes until the onions are golden brown. Stir in the cardamom pods, cinnamon stick, coriander, cumin, and turmeric and continue stirring for 2 minutes, or until the spices are aromatic.

• Add the meat to the casserole and cook, stirring occasionally, for about 5 minutes until it is brown on all sides and the fat begins to separate. Stir in the water and bring to a boil, still stirring. Reduce the heat to its lowest setting, cover the pan tightly, and simmer for 40 minutes, or until the meat is tender.

• When the lamb is tender, stir the cream and ground almonds together in a bowl. Beat in 6 tablespoons of the hot cooking liquid from the pan, then gradually beat this mixture back into the casserole. Stir in the salt and garam masala. Continue to simmer for an additional 5 minutes, uncovered, stirring occasionally.

• Garnish with a sprinkling of paprika and toasted slivered almonds to serve.

SERVES 4–6

2 tbsp vegetable or peanut oil

1 onion, coarsely chopped

2 garlic cloves, chopped

1 lb/450 g pork fillet, thickly sliced

1 red bell pepper, seeded and cut
   into squares

6 oz/175 g mushrooms, quartered

2 tbsp Thai Red Curry Paste

4 oz/115 g creamed coconut,
   chopped

1¼ cups hot pork or vegetable stock

2 tbsp Thai soy sauce

4 tomatoes, peeled, seeded, and
   chopped

handful of fresh cilantro, chopped

Red Curry Pork with Bell Peppers

To peel the tomatoes, use a sharp knife to mark a cross on the bottom of each, then place in a heatproof bowl, and cover with boiling water. Let stand for 5 minutes, rinse under cold water, and peel off the skins. Quarter, seed, and chop the flesh.

• Heat the oil in a large skillet or wok. Add the onion and garlic and cook for 1–2 minutes, or until softened but not browned.

• Add the pork slices and stir-fry for 2–3 minutes until browned all over. Add the bell pepper, mushrooms, and Thai Red Curry Paste.

• Dissolve the coconut in the hot stock and add to the wok with the soy sauce. Bring to a boil, then reduce the heat and simmer for 4–5 minutes until the liquid has reduced and thickened.

• Add the tomatoes and cilantro and cook for 1–2 minutes before serving.

SERVES 4–6

4 tbsp mustard oil

2 large onions, finely chopped

6 fresh bay leaves

6 cloves

6 garlic cloves, chopped

3 green cardamom pods, lightly
    crushed

1–2 small fresh red chilies, chopped

2 tbsp ground cumin

½ tsp salt

½ tsp ground turmeric

2 tbsp apple cider vinegar

2 tbsp water

1 tbsp tomato paste

1 lb 9 oz/700 g boneless shoulder
    of pork, trimmed and cut into
    2-inch/5-cm cubes

Pork Vindaloo

The first Europeans to invade India were the Portuguese, and it was in Goa, a state in south-western India, that they established themselves. Vindaloo comes from Goa, and takes its name from the Portuguese words for "vinegar" and "garlic."

• Heat the mustard oil in a large skillet or pan with a tight-fitting lid over high heat until it smokes. Turn off the heat and let the mustard oil cool completely.

• Reheat the mustard oil over medium-high heat. Add the onions and cook, stirring frequently, for 5–8 minutes until soft but not colored.

• Add the bay leaves, cloves, garlic, cardamom pods, chilies, cumin, salt, turmeric, and 1 tablespoon of the vinegar to the onion and stir. Stir in the water, then cover the pan and simmer for about 1 minute, or until the water is absorbed and the fat separates.

• Dissolve the tomato paste in the remaining tablespoon of vinegar, then stir it into the pan. Add the pork and stir. Add just enough water to cover the pork and bring to a boil. Reduce the heat to its lowest level, cover the pan tightly, and simmer for 40–60 minutes until the pork is tender.

• If too much liquid remains in the pan when the pork is tender, use a slotted spoon to remove the pork from the pan and boil the liquid rapidly until it reduces to the required amount. Return the pork to heat through and adjust the seasoning before serving, if necessary.

SERVES 4–6

4 tbsp ghee or vegetable or peanut oil

8 skinless, boneless chicken thighs,
    sliced

1 large onion, chopped

2 tbsp Garlic and Ginger Paste

2 green bell peppers, seeded and
    chopped

1 large fresh green chili, seeded
    and finely chopped

1 tsp ground cumin

1 tsp ground coriander

1/4–1/2 tsp chili powder

1/2 tsp ground turmeric

1/4 tsp salt

14 oz/400 g canned chopped
    tomatoes

1/2 cup water

TO GARNISH

chopped fresh cilantro

whole green chilies

Chicken Jalfrezi

To make this into a more filling meal that doesn't need any accompanying rice, add 14 oz/400 g chopped new potatoes with the tomatoes and water. Bring to a boil, then reduce the heat and simmer for 5 minutes before you add the chicken.

• Melt half the ghee in a karahi, wok, or large skillet over medium-high heat. Add the chicken pieces and cook, stirring frequently, for 5 minutes until browned but not necessarily cooked through. Remove from the pan with a slotted spoon and reserve.

• Melt the remaining ghee in the pan. Add the onion and cook, stirring frequently, for 5–8 minutes until golden brown. Stir in the Garlic and Ginger Paste and continue cooking for 2 minutes, stirring frequently. Add the bell peppers to the pan and cook for 2 minutes.

• Stir in the finely chopped chili to taste, cumin, coriander, chili powder, turmeric, and salt. Add the tomatoes with their juices and the water and bring to a boil.

• Reduce the heat to low, add the chicken, and let simmer, uncovered, for 10 minutes, stirring frequently, until the bell peppers are tender, the chicken is cooked through, and the juices run clear if you pierce a few pieces with the tip of a knife. Serve sprinkled with the chopped cilantro and garnished with whole chilies.

SERVES 4

1 chicken, weighing 3 lb 5 oz/1.5 kg,
   skinned
½ lemon
1 tsp salt
2 tbsp ghee, melted

TANDOORI MASALA PASTE

1 tbsp Garlic and Ginger Paste
1 tbsp ground paprika
1 tsp ground cinnamon
1 tsp ground cumin
½ tsp ground coriander
¼ tsp chili powder, ideally Kashmiri
   chili powder
pinch of ground cloves

¼ tsp edible red food coloring
   (optional)
few drops of edible yellow food
   coloring (optional)
generous ¾ cup plain yogurt

TO GARNISH

handful of fresh cilantro sprigs
lemon wedges

Tandoori Chicken

For a quicker version, use chicken breasts, thighs, or drumsticks. Marinate as above, preheat the oven to 450°F/230°C, and roast for 40 minutes, or until cooked through.

• To make the Tandoori Masala Paste, combine the Garlic and Ginger Paste, dry spices, and food coloring, if using, in a bowl and stir in the yogurt. You can use the paste now or store it in an airtight container in the refrigerator for up to 3 days.

• Use a small knife to make thin cuts all over the chicken. Rub the lemon half all over the chicken, then rub the salt into the cuts.

• Put the chicken in a deep bowl, add the paste, and use your hands to rub it all over the bird and into the cuts. Cover the bowl with plastic wrap and let chill in the refrigerator for at least 4 hours, but ideally up to 24 hours.

• When you are ready to cook the chicken, preheat the oven to 400°F/200°C. Put the chicken on a rack in a roasting pan, breast-side up, and dribble with the melted ghee. Roast for 45 minutes, then quickly remove the bird and roasting pan from the oven and turn the temperature to its highest setting.

• Very carefully pour out any fat from the bottom of the roasting pan. Return the chicken to the oven and roast for an additional 10–15 minutes, or until the chicken's juices run clear when you pierce the thigh with a knife and the paste is lightly charred.

• Let stand for 10 minutes, then garnish with cilantro sprigs and lemon wedges and serve, carved into pieces.

SERVES 4–6

14 oz/400 g canned chopped
  tomatoes
1¼ cups heavy cream
8 pieces cooked Tandoori Chicken
fresh cilantro sprigs, to garnish

TIKKA MASALA

2 tbsp ghee or vegetable or peanut oil
1 large garlic clove, finely chopped
1 fresh red chili, seeded and chopped
2 tsp ground cumin
2 tsp ground paprika
½ tsp salt
pepper

Chicken Tikka Masala

Using the Tandoori chicken of the preceding recipe and combining it with a rich tomato sauce transforms this dish into one of today's most popular curries—even if it is a fairly recent restaurateur's invention!

• To make the Tikka Masala, melt the ghee in a large skillet with a tight-fitting lid over medium heat. Add the garlic and chili and stir-fry for 1 minute. Stir in the cumin, paprika, salt, and pepper to taste and continue stir-frying for about 30 seconds.

• Stir the tomatoes with their juices and the cream into the pan. Reduce the heat to low and let the sauce simmer for about 10 minutes, stirring frequently, until it reduces and thickens.

• Meanwhile, remove all the bones and any skin from the Tandoori Chicken pieces, then cut the meat into bite-size pieces.

• Adjust the seasoning of the sauce, if necessary. Add the chicken pieces to the pan, cover, and let simmer for 3–5 minutes, or until the chicken is heated through. Garnish with cilantro sprigs and serve.

Fish and seafood is plentiful in India's numerous rivers, lakes, and in the sea, which surrounds it on three sides. The waters of Thailand's enormous coastline also provide a rich source of fish. For this reason, recipes for fish curries are plentiful. The most popular fresh fish in India and Thailand is butterfish, which is not dissimilar to plaice in shape, and other favorites include catfish, red snapper, king mackerel, and Thai mackerel. Shrimp and mussels are the two most popular shellfish.

Goa, the tiny Indian state south of Mumbai (Bombay), has an incredible range of seafood recipes which use fresh fish, crab, lobster, and jumbo shrimp, and is known for its spicy fish coconut curries. In fact, this style of cooking curries is frequently used in Thailand, Malaysia, and Indonesia, but seldom in other parts of India. The recipe for Shrimp with Scallions and Straw

SEA IS FOR CURRIES

Mushrooms is a perfect example of this style of cooking, as is Goan-Style Seafood Curry, which is made up of white fish such as cod and shrimp. Goa was under Portuguese occupancy for over four hundred and fifty years and so its cooking has a marked Portuguese influence.

Finally, a few words on Bombay duck. This is actually a fish, which is found in quantity in the rivers around Mumbai. It is filleted, dried in the sun, and stored in jars. Use it crumbled over your curry as a garnish, but be warned—it is an acquired taste!

SERVES 4

2 tbsp vegetable or peanut oil

1 large onion, chopped

2 garlic cloves, chopped

3 oz/85 g white mushrooms

8 oz/225 g angler fish, cut into
1-inch/2.5-cm cubes

8 oz/225 g salmon fillets, cut into
1-inch/2.5-cm cubes

8 oz/225 g cod, cut into 1-inch/2.5-cm
cubes

2 tbsp Thai Red Curry Paste

1¾ cups canned coconut milk

handful of fresh cilantro, chopped

1 tsp palm sugar or brown sugar

1 tsp Thai fish sauce

4 oz/115 g rice noodles

3 scallions, chopped

1 cup bean sprouts

few fresh Thai basil leaves,
to garnish

Fish Curry with Rice Noodles

Coconut milk is used frequently in Thai curries to flavor and enrich them. It is not, however, as one might think, the liquid inside the coconut. Coconut milk is actually made from the flesh of fresh coconut, which is grated and pressed and then combined with water.

• Heat the oil in a large skillet or wok. Add the onion, garlic, and mushrooms and gently cook until softened but not browned.

• Add the fish, Thai Red Curry Paste, and coconut milk and bring gently to a boil. Simmer for 2–3 minutes before adding half the cilantro, the sugar, and fish sauce. Keep warm.

• Meanwhile, soak the rice noodles for 3–4 minutes (check the package directions), or until tender, and drain well using a colander. Put the colander and noodles over a pan of simmering water. Add the scallions, bean sprouts, and most of the basil leaves and steam on top of the noodles for 1–2 minutes, or until just wilted.

• Pile the noodles onto warmed serving plates and top with the fish curry. Scatter the remaining cilantro over the top, garnish with basil, and serve immediately.

SERVES 4–6

2 lb/900 g thick fish fillets, such as angler fish, red snapper, cod, or haddock, rinsed and cut into large chunks

2 fresh bay leaves, torn

²/₃ cup ghee or vegetable or peanut oil

2 large onions, chopped

½ tbsp salt

²/₃ cup water

fresh cilantro sprigs, to garnish

MARINADE

½ tbsp Garlic and Ginger Paste

1 fresh green chili, seeded and chopped

1 tsp ground coriander

1 tsp ground cumin

½ tsp ground turmeric

¼–½ tsp chili powder

1 tbsp water

salt

Balti Fish Curry

Do not overbrown the onions or the dish will taste bitter. They should be golden, but not brown, when the fish is added.

• To make the marinade, mix the Garlic and Ginger Paste, green chili, coriander, cumin, turmeric, and chili powder together with salt to taste in a large bowl. Gradually stir in the water to form a thin paste. Add the fish chunks and smear with the marinade. Tuck the bay leaves underneath, cover, and let marinate in the refrigerator for at least 30 minutes, or up to 4 hours.

• Remove the fish from the refrigerator 15 minutes before you intend to start cooking. Melt the ghee in a karahi, wok, or large skillet over medium-high heat. Add the onions, sprinkle with the salt, and cook, stirring frequently, for 8 minutes, or until very soft and golden.

• Gently add the fish and bay leaves to the pan and stir in the water. Bring to a boil, then immediately reduce the heat and cook the fish, spooning the sauce over the fish and carefully moving the chunks around, for 4–5 minutes until they are cooked through and the flesh flakes easily. Adjust the seasoning, if necessary, and garnish with cilantro sprigs.

SERVES 4–6

4 tbsp Thai fish sauce

2 tbsp Thai soy sauce

1 fresh red chili, seeded and chopped

12 oz/350 g angler fish fillet, cut into cubes

12 oz/350 g salmon fillets, skinned and cut into cubes

juice of 1 lime

1¾ cups canned coconut milk

3 kaffir lime leaves

1 tbsp Thai Red Curry Paste

1 lemon grass stalk (white part only), finely chopped

Fish Curry

Angler fish and salmon lend themselves well to this richly flavored dish, but you could use just one of these fish. Another alternative, to be truly authentic, would be to use butterfish, which is one of the most popular fish in Thailand.

• Combine half the fish sauce and the soy sauce in a shallow, non-metallic dish. Add the chili and fish, squeeze over the lime, and stir to coat. Cover and chill for 1–2 hours, or overnight.

• Bring the coconut milk to a boil in a pan and add the lime leaves, Thai Red Curry Paste, the remaining fish sauce, and the lemon grass. Simmer gently for 10–15 minutes.

• Add the fish and the marinade and simmer gently for a further 4–5 minutes, or until the fish is cooked. Serve hot.

SERVES 4–6

2 tbsp vegetable or peanut oil

6 scallions, coarsely chopped

1-inch/2.5-cm piece fresh gingerroot, grated

2–3 tbsp Thai Red Curry Paste

1¾ cups canned coconut milk

⅔ cup fish stock

4 kaffir lime leaves

1 lemon grass stalk, broken in half

12 oz/350 g white fish fillets, skinned and cut into chunks

8 oz/225 g raw squid rings and tentacles

8 oz/225 g large cooked shelled shrimp

1 tbsp Thai fish sauce

2 tbsp Thai soy sauce

4 tbsp chopped fresh Chinese chives

Fish in Coconut

Most varieties of fish fillet suit this recipe, but firm-textured fish, such as cod and haddock, are the most suitable. Don't be tempted to stir the mixture too vigorously or the fish may fall apart.

• Heat the oil in a large skillet or wok. Add the scallions and ginger and stir-fry for 1–2 minutes. Add the Thai Red Curry Paste and stir-fry for an additional 1–2 minutes.

• Add the coconut milk, fish stock, lime leaves, and lemon grass. Bring to a boil, then reduce the heat and simmer for 1 minute.

• Add the fish, squid, and shrimp and simmer for 2–3 minutes, or until the fish is cooked. Add the fish and soy sauces and stir in the chives. Serve immediately.

SERVES 4–6

3 tbsp vegetable or peanut oil

1 tbsp black mustard seeds

12 fresh curry leaves or 1 tbsp dried

6 shallots, finely chopped

1 garlic clove, crushed

1 tsp ground turmeric

½ tsp ground coriander

¼–½ tsp chili powder

5 oz/140 g creamed coconut, grated and dissolved in 1¼ cups boiling water

1 lb 2 oz/500 g skinless, boneless white fish, such as angler fish or cod, cut into large chunks

1 lb/450 g large raw shrimp, shelled and deveined

finely grated rind and juice of 1 lime

salt

lime wedges, to garnish

Goan-style Seafood Curry

Peeling a large number of shallots like this can be fiddly, but the job is quicker if you submerge them first in a pan of boiling water for 30–45 seconds. Drain the shallots and use a knife to slice off the root end, then they should peel easily.

• Heat the oil in a karahi, wok, or large skillet over high heat. Add the mustard seeds and stir them around for about 1 minute, or until they jump. Stir in the curry leaves.

• Add the shallots and garlic and stir-fry for about 5 minutes, or until the shallots are golden. Stir in the turmeric, coriander, and chili powder and continue stir-frying for about 30 seconds.

• Add the dissolved creamed coconut. Bring to a boil, then reduce the heat to medium and cook, stirring, for about 2 minutes.

• Reduce the heat to low, add the fish, and simmer for 1 minute, stirring the sauce over the fish and very gently stirring it around. Add the shrimp and continue to simmer for 4–5 minutes until the fish flesh flakes easily and the shrimp turn pink and curl.

• Add half the lime juice, then taste and add more lime juice and salt to taste. Sprinkle the lime rind over, garnish with lime wedges, and serve.

SERVES 4–6

1 tbsp vegetable or peanut oil

3 shallots, finely chopped

1-inch/2.5-cm piece fresh galangal, thinly sliced

2 garlic cloves, finely chopped

1¾ cups canned coconut milk

2 lemon grass stalks, snapped in half

4 tbsp Thai fish sauce

2 tbsp chili sauce

8 oz/225 g raw jumbo shrimp, shelled, and deveined

8 oz/225 g raw baby squid, cleaned and thickly sliced

8 oz/225 g salmon fillet, skinned and cut into chunks

6 oz/175 g fresh tuna steak, cut into chunks

8 oz/225 g live mussels, scrubbed and debearded

fresh Chinese chives, to garnish

Mixed Seafood Curry

If you are unable to find the fresh galangal needed for this recipe, you could substitute it with fresh gingerroot, to which it is related. It is worth remembering that, when you do buy it, it can be stored in the refrigerator for about 2 weeks, or be frozen.

• Heat the oil in a large skillet or wok. Add the shallots, galangal, and garlic and stir-fry for 1–2 minutes, or until they start to soften. Add the coconut milk, lemon grass, fish sauce, and chili sauce. Bring to a boil, then reduce the heat, and simmer for an additional 1–2 minutes.

• Add the shrimp, squid, salmon, and tuna and simmer for 3–4 minutes, or until the shrimp have turned pink and the fish is cooked.

• Add the mussels and cover with a lid. Simmer for 1–2 minutes until they have opened. Discard any mussels that remain closed. Garnish with Chinese chives and serve immediately.

SERVES 4–6

1 tbsp vegetable or peanut oil

3 shallots, chopped

1 fresh red chili, seeded and chopped

1 tbsp Thai Red Curry Paste

1 lemon grass stalk (white part only),
  finely chopped

8 oz/225 g cooked shelled shrimp

14 oz/400 g canned straw
  mushrooms, drained

2 tbsp Thai fish sauce

2 tbsp Thai soy sauce

8 oz/225 g fresh egg noodles

chopped fresh cilantro, to garnish

Curried Noodles with Shrimp and Straw Mushrooms

This is a dish to make when you are in a hurry, because it only takes about 15 minutes to prepare and cook from start to finish, if you have a store of Red Curry Paste. If time is really at a premium, even that can be bought in Asian markets, along with the straw mushrooms.

• Heat the oil in a large skillet or wok. Add the shallots and chili and stir-fry for 2–3 minutes. Add the Thai Red Curry Paste and lemon grass and stir-fry for an additional 2–3 minutes.

• Add the shrimp, mushrooms, fish sauce, and soy sauce and stir well to mix.

• Meanwhile, cook the noodles in boiling water for 3–4 minutes, drain, and transfer to warmed plates. Top with the shrimp curry, sprinkle the cilantro over, and serve immediately.

SERVES 4–6

2 tbsp vegetable or peanut oil

bunch of scallions, chopped, plus
    whole scallions, to garnish

2 garlic cloves, finely chopped

6 oz/175 g creamed coconut, coarsely
    chopped

2 tbsp Thai Red Curry Paste

generous 1¾ cups fish stock

2 tbsp Thai fish sauce

2 tbsp Thai soy sauce

6 fresh Thai basil sprigs

14 oz/400 g canned straw
    mushrooms, drained

12 oz/350 g large cooked shelled
    shrimp

Shrimp with Scallions and Straw Mushrooms

Shrimp in a curry sauce is a popular Thai dish, and although here they are cooked in Red Curry Paste, if you prefer them slightly hotter, you could use Green Curry Paste.

• Heat the oil in a large skillet or wok. Add the scallions and garlic and stir-fry for 2–3 minutes. Add the creamed coconut, Thai Red Curry Paste, and stock, and heat gently until the coconut has dissolved.

• Stir in the fish sauce and soy sauce, then add the basil, mushrooms, and shrimp. Gradually bring to a boil, then transfer the curry to individual serving bowls, garnish with scallions, and serve immediately.

SERVES 4–6

4 tbsp plain yogurt

2 fresh green chilies, seeded and
chopped

½ tbsp Garlic and Ginger Paste

seeds from 4 green cardamom pods

2 tsp ground cumin

1 tsp tomato paste

¼ tsp ground turmeric

¼ tsp salt

pinch of chili powder, ideally Kashmiri
chili powder

24 raw jumbo shrimp, shelled,
deveined, and tails left intact

vegetable or peanut oil

lemon or lime wedges, to garnish

Tandoori Shrimp

This spiced yogurt mixture also makes an excellent marinade for tandoori seafood kabobs made of meaty fillets of white fish, such as cod, halibut, or angler fish.

• Put the yogurt, chilies, and Garlic and Ginger Paste in a food processor or blender and process to form a paste, or crush using a pestle and mortar. Transfer the paste to a large, non-metallic bowl and stir in the cardamom seeds, cumin, tomato paste, turmeric, salt, and chili powder.

• Add the shrimp to the bowl and use your hands to make sure they are thoroughly coated with the yogurt and spice mixture. Cover the bowl with plastic wrap and let marinate in the refrigerator for at least 30 minutes, or up to 4 hours.

• When you are ready to cook, heat a large, flat tava, griddle, or skillet over high heat until a splash of water "dances" when it hits the surface. Use crumpled paper towels or a pastry brush to very lightly coat the hot pan with oil.

• Use tongs to lift the shrimp out of the marinade, letting the excess drip back into the bowl, then place the shrimp on the tava and let them cook for 2 minutes. Flip the shrimp over and cook for an additional 1–2 minutes until they turn pink, curl, and appear opaque all the way through. Garnish with lemon or lime wedges and serve.

A large proportion of the population of India, especially in the south, is vegetarian. In fact, the total could be in excess of three-quarters of the population. Influences contributing to this factor include those of Buddha, the founder of Buddhism, Mahavir, the founder of Jainism, and the powerful and popular King Ashoka, born in 304 BC, who all believed in not killing animals.

Fortunately, the variety of fresh vegetables available in India is plentiful and it therefore stands to reason that there are many imaginative ways in which Indians cook them, from potato dishes, such as Aloo Gobi and Sag Aloo, to Zucchini and Cashew Nut Curry and Carrot and Pumpkin Curry. It is thought that the variety of vegetarian dishes from India is the largest in the world. If you think of all the different vegetables, the variety of spices available, and the different cooking styles, and put them

VITALLY VEGETARIAN

together, you begin to realize the numerous permutations that are possible. Vegetables are often cooked in coconut milk, particularly in Thai curries, as you can see in the recipes for Vegetables with Tofu and Spinach, and Green Beans with Mustard Seeds and Coconut.

Serve these vegetarian dishes as an entrée with bread or rice, and yogurt, which is traditionally always served with a vegetarian curry in some form or other. If you wish to serve these dishes as an accompaniment, then they will obviously serve more—unless you give in to the temptation to eat more than an average portion, that is!

SERVES 4

2/3 cup vegetable stock

1-inch/2.5-cm piece fresh galangal, sliced

2 garlic cloves, chopped

1 lemon grass stalk (white part only), finely chopped

2 fresh red chilies, seeded and chopped

4 carrots, peeled and cut into chunks

8 oz/225 g pumpkin, peeled, seeded, and cut into cubes

2 tbsp vegetable or peanut oil

2 shallots, finely chopped

3 tbsp Thai Yellow Curry Paste

1¾ cups canned coconut milk

4–6 fresh Thai basil sprigs

¼ cup toasted pumpkin seeds, to garnish

Carrot and Pumpkin Curry

When pumpkins are not available, use butternut squash instead. Peel, remove the seeds, and cut into cubes before cooking.

• Pour the stock into a large pan and bring to a boil. Add the galangal, half the garlic, the lemon grass, and chilies and simmer for 5 minutes. Add the carrots and pumpkin and simmer for 5–6 minutes, or until tender.

• Heat the oil in a large skillet or wok. Add the shallots and the remaining garlic and stir-fry for 2–3 minutes. Add the Thai Yellow Curry Paste and stir-fry for an additional 1–2 minutes.

• Stir the shallot mixture into the pan containing the pumpkin and add the coconut milk and basil. Simmer for 2–3 minutes. Serve hot, sprinkled with the toasted pumpkin seeds.

SERVES 4

2 tbsp vegetable or peanut oil

6 scallions, chopped

2 garlic cloves, chopped

2 fresh green chilies, seeded
   and chopped

1 lb/450 g zucchini, cut into
   thick slices

4 oz/115 g shiitake mushrooms,
   halved

1 cup bean sprouts

scant 2/3 cup cashew nuts, toasted
   or dry-fried

few Chinese chives, chopped, plus
   whole chive lengths to garnish

4 tbsp Thai soy sauce

1 tsp Thai fish sauce (optional)

Zucchini and Cashew Nut Curry

Try to find small zucchini.
If you have to use larger
ones you may need to
cut the slices in half
before cooking.

• Heat the oil in a large skillet or wok. Add the scallions, garlic, and chilies and cook for 1–2 minutes until softened but not browned.

• Add the zucchini and mushrooms and cook for 2–3 minutes until tender.

• Add the bean sprouts, nuts, chives, the soy sauce, and the fish sauce, if using, and stir-fry for 1–2 minutes.

• Garnish with whole chive lengths and serve the curry immediately.

SERVES 4

scant 2/3 cup cashew nuts

1½ tbsp Garlic and Ginger Paste

generous ¾ cup water

4 tbsp ghee or vegetable or peanut oil

1 large onion, chopped

5 green cardamom pods, lightly
crushed

1 cinnamon stick, broken in half

¼ tsp ground turmeric

generous 1 cup heavy cream

5 oz/140 g new potatoes, scrubbed
and chopped into ½-inch/1-cm
pieces

5 oz/140 g cauliflower florets

½ tsp garam masala

5 oz/140 g eggplant, chopped into
chunks

5 oz/140 g green beans, chopped
into ½-inch/1-cm pieces

salt and pepper

chopped fresh mint or cilantro,
to garnish

Cauliflower, Eggplant, and Green Bean Korma

When serving this dish,
remember to tell guests
that it contains cardamom
pods, which have a bitter
taste if bitten.

• Heat a large flameproof casserole or skillet with a tight-fitting lid over high heat. Add the cashew nuts and dry-fry, stirring constantly, until just starting to brown, then immediately tip them out of the casserole.

• Put the nuts in a small food processor or blender with the Garlic and Ginger Paste and 1 tablespoon of the water and whiz until a coarse paste forms.

• Melt half the ghee in the casserole over medium-high heat. Add the onion and cook for 5–8 minutes until they are golden brown.

• Add the nut paste and stir-fry for 5 minutes. Stir in the cardamom pods, cinnamon stick, and turmeric.

• Add the cream and remaining water and bring to a boil, stirring. Reduce the heat to the lowest level, cover the casserole, and simmer for 5 minutes.

• Add the potatoes, cauliflower, and garam masala and simmer, covered, for 5 minutes. Stir in the eggplant and green beans and continue simmering for an additional 5 minutes, or until all the vegetables are tender. Check the sauce occasionally to make sure it isn't sticking to the bottom of the pan, and stir in a little extra water if needed.

• Taste and add seasoning, if necessary. Garnish with mint and serve.

SERVES 4

2 tbsp vegetable or peanut oil

1 onion, chopped

2 garlic cloves, crushed

2 fresh red chilies, seeded and
    chopped

1 tbsp Thai Red Curry Paste

1 large eggplant, cut into chunks

4 oz/115 g pea eggplants or chopped
    eggplant

4 oz/115 g baby fava beans

4 oz/115 g fine green beans

1¼ cups vegetable stock

2 oz/55 g creamed coconut, chopped

3 tbsp Thai soy sauce

1 tsp palm sugar or brown sugar

3 kaffir lime leaves, coarsely torn

4 tbsp chopped fresh cilantro

Eggplant and Bean Curry

Look for the pea
eggplants, which are
very popular in Thai
cooking, but if you cannot
find them, just use the
more familiar purple ones.

• Heat the oil in a large skillet or wok. Add the onion, garlic, and chilies and cook for 1–2 minutes. Stir in the Thai Red Curry Paste and cook for an additional 1–2 minutes.

• Add all the eggplants and cook for 3–4 minutes, or until starting to soften. (You may need to add a little more oil, as eggplants soak it up quickly.) Add all the beans and stir-fry for 2 minutes.

• Pour in the stock and add the creamed coconut, soy sauce, sugar, and lime leaves. Bring gently to a boil and cook until the coconut has dissolved. Stir in the cilantro and serve hot.

SERVES 4

8 oz/225 g firm tofu, drained and cut
    into cubes
2 tbsp vegetable or peanut oil, plus
    extra for deep frying
2 onions, chopped
2 garlic cloves, chopped
1 fresh red chili, seeded and sliced
3 celery stalks, diagonally sliced

8 oz/225 g mushrooms, thickly sliced
4 oz/115 g baby corn, cut in half
1 red bell pepper, seeded and cut
    into strips
3 tbsp Thai Red Curry Paste
1¾ cups canned coconut milk
1 tsp palm sugar or brown sugar
2 tbsp Thai soy sauce
8 oz/225 g fresh baby spinach leaves

Vegetables with Tofu and Spinach

Tofu, or bean curd, is used extensively in Thailand, and because it is so nutritious, high in protein, low in calories, and vegetable based, it is ideal for vegetarians. It is delicate and will fall apart if cooked too long or stirred too frequently, so deep-frying it, as in this recipe, is the perfect answer.

• Heat enough oil in a skillet to deep-fry the tofu cubes, in batches, for 4–5 minutes, or until crisp and browned. Remove with a slotted spoon and drain on paper towels.

• Heat 2 tablespoons of oil in a large skillet or wok. Add the onions, garlic, and chili and stir-fry for 1–2 minutes, or until they start to soften. Add the celery, mushrooms, baby corn, and red bell pepper and stir-fry for 3–4 minutes, or until they soften.

• Stir in the curry paste and coconut milk and gradually bring to a boil. Add the sugar and soy sauce and then the spinach. Cook, stirring constantly, until the spinach has wilted. Serve immediately, topped with the tofu.

Chili-Yogurt Mushrooms

SERVES 4

4 tbsp ghee or vegetable or peanut oil	½ tsp chili powder
2 large onions, chopped	1 lb 10 oz/750 g cremini mushrooms, thickly sliced
4 large garlic cloves, crushed	pinch of sugar
14 oz/400 g canned chopped tomatoes	salt
1 tsp ground turmeric	½ cup plain yogurt
1 tsp garam masala	chopped fresh cilantro and cilantro sprigs, to garnish

Adding the salt with the mushrooms draws out their moisture, giving extra flavor to the juices.

• Melt the ghee in a karahi, wok, or large skillet over medium-high heat. Add the onion and cook, stirring frequently, for 5–8 minutes until golden. Stir in the garlic and stir-fry for an additional 2 minutes.

• Add the tomatoes and their juices and mix together. Stir in the turmeric, garam masala, and chili powder and continue cooking for an additional 3 minutes.

• Add the mushrooms, sugar, and salt to taste and cook for 8 minutes, or until they have given off their liquid and are soft and tender.

• Turn off the heat, then stir in the yogurt, a little at a time, beating vigorously to prevent it curdling. Taste and adjust the seasoning, if necessary. Garnish with cilantro and serve.

Sag Aloo

Mustard seeds are most commonly used for flavoring vegetable dishes and dals. They have a slightly nutty taste that is released on being cooked in hot oil.

SERVES 4

1 lb 2 oz/500 g fresh spinach leaves

2 tbsp ghee or vegetable oil

1 tsp black mustard seeds

1 onion, halved and sliced

2 tsp Garlic and Ginger Paste

2 lb/900 g waxy potatoes, cut into small chunks

1 tsp chili powder

½ cup vegetable stock or water

salt

• Bring a large pan of water to a boil. Add the spinach leaves and blanch for 4 minutes. Drain well, then tip in to a clean dish towel, roll up, and gently squeeze out the excess liquid.

• Melt the ghee in a separate pan. Add the mustard seeds and cook over low heat, stirring constantly, for 2 minutes, or until they give off their aroma. Add the onion and Garlic and Ginger Paste and cook, stirring frequently, for 5 minutes, or until softened.

• Add the potatoes, chili powder, and vegetable stock and season to taste with salt. Bring to a boil, cover, and cook for 10 minutes. Add the spinach and stir it in, then cover and simmer for an additional 10 minutes, or until the potatoes are tender. Serve immediately.

Green Beans with Mustard Seeds and Coconut

SERVES 4

3 tbsp ghee or vegetable or peanut oil

1 tbsp mustard seeds

6 fresh curry leaves or ½ tbsp dried

1 onion, chopped

½ tbsp Garlic and Ginger Paste

pinch of ground turmeric

1 lb/450 g green beans, chopped

2 oz/55 g creamed coconut, grated

generous 1 cup water

salt and pepper

pinch of chili powder or paprika,
to garnish

• Melt the ghee in a karahi, wok, or large skillet over high heat. Add the mustard seeds and stir around for about a minute until they pop. Stir in the curry leaves.

• Add the onion, Garlic and Ginger Paste, and turmeric and stir-fry for 5 minutes. Add the green beans and stir-fry for 2 minutes.

• Sprinkle in the creamed coconut, then add the water and bring to a boil, stirring. Reduce the heat to low and simmer, stirring occasionally, for about 4 minutes until the beans are tender, but still have some bite. Taste and adjust the seasoning and serve sprinkled with a little chili powder to garnish.

If you like your vegetable dishes with more heat, add 1 chopped fresh green chili with the Garlic and Ginger Paste.

SERVES 4

4 tbsp ghee or vegetable or peanut oil

½ tbsp cumin seeds

1 onion, chopped

1½-inch/4-cm piece fresh gingerroot,
    finely chopped

1 fresh green chili, seeded and
    thinly sliced

1 lb/450 g cauliflower, cut into
    small florets

1 lb/450 g large waxy potatoes,
    peeled and cut into large chunks

½ tsp ground coriander

½ tsp garam masala

¼ tsp salt, or to taste

fresh cilantro sprigs, to garnish

Aloo Gobi

For a more golden-colored dish, add a quarter teaspoon of ground turmeric with the other ground spices.

• Melt the ghee in a flameproof casserole or large skillet with a tight-fitting lid over medium-high heat. Add the cumin seeds and stir around for about 30 seconds until they crackle and start to brown.

• Immediately stir in the onion, ginger, and chili and stir-fry for 5–8 minutes until the onion is golden brown.

• Stir in the cauliflower and potato, followed by the coriander, garam masala, and salt to taste, and continue stir-frying for about 30 seconds.

• Cover the pan, reduce the heat to the lowest setting, and simmer, stirring occasionally, for 20–30 minutes until the vegetables are tender when pierced with the point of a knife. Check occasionally that they aren't sticking to the bottom of the pan and stir in a little water, if necessary.

• Taste and adjust the seasoning, if necessary, and garnish with cilantro sprigs to serve.

Traditionally, in India, curry is always served with bread and/or rice, a yogurt relish (Raita), and chutney or a relish of finely chopped fresh vegetable salad. The idea is that the bread is used to scoop up the curry for eating, and as most Indian breads are unleavened and therefore flat, they are ideal for this use. The two favorites are Naan Bread and Chapattis, the recipes for which can be found in this chapter. In Thailand, curries are centered on rice and are accompanied with a dipping sauce and a selection of raw and blanched vegetables. Basmati rice is the favorite choice in India, as it is grown in India and Pakistan, with the best quality grown in the foothills of the Indian Himalayas. This is a long-grain rice with a delicate flavor and is ideal for eating with curry gravy. It can be served plain boiled, spiced, or with additional ingredients, as in Fruit and Nut Pilaf. In Thailand, there are

BITE ON THE SIDE

two main varieties of rice available. Thai fragrant rice is served most frequently. It is a long-grain rice scented with jasmine and is light and fluffy when cooked. Sticky or glutinous rice is commonly served in the north of the country. It is a short-grain rice that, as its name suggests, is sticky and thick when cooked.

Raita and chutney are indispensable accompaniments to an Indian curry. Raita, which is based on yogurt and a vegetable or herb, such as cucumber or mint, is refreshing and helps to cool down a hot spicy curry. The chutney you choose to serve is a matter of personal choice, but Mango Chutney is always popular!

MAKES 10

6 cups white bread flour

1 tbsp baking powder

1 tsp sugar

1 tsp salt

1¼ cups water, heated to 122°F/50°C

1 egg, beaten

4 tbsp melted ghee or vegetable oil,
   plus a little extra for rolling out,
   oiling, and brushing

fresh cilantro sprigs, to garnish

Naan Bread

To make garlic and nigella seed naans, scatter the dough just before it is baked with 3 very thinly sliced garlic cloves and 2 tablespoons nigella seeds. For sesame naans, sprinkle the dough just before it is baked with 2 tablespoons sesame seeds. For cilantro naans, knead 2 oz/55 g finely chopped fresh cilantro into the dough after the ghee has been incorporated.

• Sift the flour, baking powder, sugar, and salt into a large mixing bowl and make a well in the center. Mix the water and egg together, beating until the egg breaks up and is blended with the liquid.

• Slowly add the liquid mixture to the well in the dry ingredients, using your fingers to draw in the flour from the side, until a stiff, heavy dough forms. Shape the dough into a ball and return it to the bowl.

• Soak a clean dish towel in hot water, then wring it out and use it to cover the bowl, tucking the ends of the dish towel under the bowl. Let the dough rest for 30 minutes.

• Turn out the dough onto a counter brushed with melted ghee and flatten with a rolling pin. Gradually sprinkle the dough with the melted ghee and knead to work it in, little by little, until it is completely incorporated. Shape the dough into 10 equal balls.

• Resoak the dish towel in hot water and wring it out again, then place it over the dough balls and let them rest and rise for 1 hour.

• Meanwhile, put 1 or 2 cookie sheets in the oven and preheat the oven to 450°F/230°C or its highest setting.

• Use a lightly greased rolling pin to roll the dough balls into teardrop shapes, about ⅛ inch/3 mm thick. Use crumpled paper towels to rub the hot cookie sheets lightly with ghee. Arrange the naans on the cookie sheets and bake for 5–6 minutes until they are golden brown and lightly puffed. As you take the naans out of the oven, brush with melted ghee and serve immediately, garnished with cilantro.

MAKES 6

1⅓ cups whole wheat flour, sifted,
    plus extra for dusting
½ tsp salt
⅔–¾ cup water
melted ghee or vegetable oil, for
    brushing

Chapattis

Do not be tempted to flip the chapattis more times than specified above, or they will not puff up and will become heavy. Indian cooks use their fingers to flip the dough over, but use a pair of tongs or a metal spatula if you want to.

• Mix the flour and salt together in a large bowl and make a well in the center. Gradually stir in enough water to make a stiff dough.
• Turn out the dough onto a lightly floured counter and knead for 10 minutes, or until it is smooth and elastic. Shape the dough into a ball and place it in the cleaned bowl, then cover with a damp dish towel and let rest for 20 minutes.
• Divide the dough into 6 equal pieces. Lightly flour your hands and roll each piece of dough into a ball. Meanwhile, heat a large, ungreased tava, skillet, or griddle over high heat until very hot and a splash of water "dances" when it hits the surface.
• Working with 1 ball of dough at a time, flatten the dough between your palms, then roll it out on a lightly floured counter into a 7-inch/18-cm circle. Slap the dough onto the hot pan and cook until brown flecks appear on the bottom. Flip the dough over and repeat on the other side.
• Flip the dough over again and use a bunched up dish towel to press down all around the edge. This pushes around the steam in the chapatti, causing the chapatti to puff up. Continue cooking until the bottom is golden brown, then flip over and repeat this step on the other side.
• Brush the chapatti with melted ghee and serve, then repeat with the remaining dough balls. Chapattis are best served immediately, as soon as they come out of the pan, but they can be kept warm, wrapped in foil, for 20 minutes.

SERVES 4–6

generous 1 cup basmati rice

2 tbsp ghee or vegetable or peanut oil

5 green cardamom pods, lightly
     crushed

5 cloves

2 fresh bay leaves

½ cinnamon stick

1 tsp fennel seeds

½ tsp black mustard seeds

scant 2 cups water

1½ tsp salt

2 tbsp chopped fresh cilantro

pepper

Spiced Basmati Rice

To make spiced saffron basmati rice, lightly toast 1 teaspoon saffron threads in a dry skillet over medium-high heat until you can smell the aroma, then immediately tip them out of the pan. Bring the water to a boil while the rice soaks, stir in the saffron threads and the salt, and let infuse. Follow the recipe as above, replacing the plain water with the golden saffron-flavored water.

• Rinse the basmati rice in several changes of water until the water runs clear, then let soak for 30 minutes. Drain and reserve until ready to cook.

• Melt the ghee in a flameproof casserole or large pan with a tight-fitting lid over medium-high heat. Add the spices and stir-fry for 30 seconds. Stir the rice into the casserole so that the grains are coated with ghee. Stir in the water and salt and bring to a boil.

• Reduce the heat to as low as possible and cover the casserole tightly. Simmer, without lifting the lid, for 8–10 minutes until the grains are tender and all the liquid is absorbed.

• Turn off the heat and use 2 forks to mix the cilantro into the rice. Adjust the seasoning, if necessary. Re-cover the pan and let stand for 5 minutes.

SERVES 4–6

generous 1 cup basmati rice

scant 2 cups water

½ tsp saffron threads

1 tsp salt

2 tbsp ghee or vegetable or peanut oil

generous ⅓ cup blanched almonds

1 onion, thinly sliced

1 cinnamon stick, broken in half

seeds from 4 green cardamom pods

1 tsp cumin seeds

1 tsp black peppercorns, lightly
  crushed

2 fresh bay leaves

3 tbsp finely chopped dried mango

3 tbsp finely chopped dried apricots

2 tbsp golden raisins

⅓ cup pistachio nuts, chopped

Fruit and Nut Pilaf

If the pilaf, or any of the other rice dishes, are ready before you want to serve, place a clean dish towel between the rice and lid and let the rice stand for up to 20 minutes after you stir in the nuts. The dish towel will absorb the steam and prevent the rice from becoming soggy.

• Rinse the basmati rice in several changes of water until the water runs clear, then let soak for 30 minutes. Drain and reserve until ready to cook.

• Boil the water in a small pan. Add the saffron threads and salt, remove from the heat, and let infuse.

• Melt the ghee in a flameproof casserole or large pan with a tight-fitting lid over medium-high heat. Add the almonds and stir-fry until golden brown, then use a slotted spoon to scoop them out immediately from the casserole and reserve until required.

• Add the onion to the casserole and cook, stirring frequently, for 5–8 minutes until golden but not brown. Add the spices and bay leaves to the pan and stir-fry for 30 seconds.

• Add the rice to the casserole and stir until the grains are coated with ghee. Add the saffron-infused water and bring to a boil. Reduce the heat to as low as possible, stir in the dried fruit, and cover the casserole tightly. Simmer, without lifting the lid, for 8–10 minutes until the grains are tender and all the liquid is absorbed.

• Turn off the heat and use 2 forks to mix the almonds and pistachios into the rice. Adjust the seasoning, if necessary. Re-cover the pan and let stand for 5 minutes.

SERVES 4–6

generous 1 cup basmati rice

scant 2 cups water

2¼ oz/60 g creamed coconut

2 tbsp mustard oil

1½ tsp salt

fresh coconut slices, to garnish

   (optional)

Coconut Rice

The mustard oil is heated and then cooled to reduce the pungency of its flavor. If you prefer to use vegetable or peanut oil, you can skip this part of the recipe.

• Rinse the basmati rice in several changes of water until the water runs clear, then let soak for 30 minutes. Drain and reserve until ready to cook.

• Bring the water to a boil in a small pan, stir in the creamed coconut until it dissolves, and reserve.

• Heat the mustard oil in a large skillet or pan with a lid over high heat until it smokes. Turn off the heat and let the mustard oil cool completely.

• When you are ready to cook, reheat the mustard oil over medium-high heat. Add the rice and stir until all the grains are coated in oil. Add the water with the dissolved coconut and bring to a boil.

• Reduce the heat to as low as possible, stir in the salt, and cover the pan tightly. Simmer, without lifting the lid, for 8–10 minutes until the grains are tender and all the liquid is absorbed.

• Turn off the heat and use 2 forks to mix the rice. Adjust the seasoning, if necessary. Re-cover the pan and let the rice stand for 5 minutes. Serve the rice garnished with coconut slices, if liked.

MAKES ABOUT 5 OZ/140 G

½ fresh coconut, about 4 oz/115 g
of meat, or 4½ oz/125 g dry
unsweetened coconut

2 fresh green chilies, seeded or not,
to taste, and chopped

1-inch/2.5-cm piece fresh gingerroot,
finely chopped

4 tbsp chopped fresh cilantro

2 tbsp lemon juice, or to taste

2 shallots, very finely chopped

Coconut Sambal

For a punchier-tasting chutney, stir in 1–2 tablespoons black mustard seeds with the shallots. A little ground cumin is also a good addition.

• If you are using a whole coconut, use a hammer and nail to punch a hole in the "eye" of the coconut, then pour out the water from the inside and reserve. Use the hammer to break the coconut in half, then peel half and chop.

• Put the coconut and chilies in a small food processor and whiz for about 30 seconds until finely chopped. Add the ginger, cilantro, and lemon juice and whiz again.

• If the mixture seems too dry, whiz in about 1 tablespoon coconut water or water. Stir in the shallots and serve immediately, or cover and chill until required. This will keep its fresh flavor, covered, in the refrigerator for up to 3 days.

SERVES 4–6
1 large piece of cucumber, about
    10½ oz/300 g, rinsed
1 tsp salt
1¾ cups plain yogurt
½ tsp sugar
pinch of ground cumin
2 tbsp chopped fresh cilantro or mint
chili powder, to garnish

Raita

For a variation, stir in 2 seeded and finely chopped tomatoes or 4 finely chopped scallions with the cilantro or mint. To make a banana raita, peel and slice 3 bananas directly into the yogurt, then stir in 2 seeded and chopped fresh green chilies and 1 tablespoon garam masala. Add a little lemon rind and juice, if you like. Cover and chill until required, then stir in the chopped fresh cilantro or mint just before serving.

• Lay a clean dish towel flat on the counter. Coarsely grate the unpeeled cucumber directly onto the dish towel. Sprinkle with half a teaspoon of the salt, then gather up the dish towel and squeeze until all the excess moisture is removed from the cucumber.

• Pour the yogurt into a bowl and beat in the remaining salt, together with the sugar and cumin. Stir in the grated cucumber. Taste and add extra seasoning, if necessary. Cover and chill until ready to serve.

• Stir in the chopped cilantro and transfer to a serving bowl. Sprinkle with chili powder and serve.

MAKES ABOUT 9 OZ/250 G

1 large mango, about 14 oz/400 g,
    peeled, pitted, and finely chopped

2 tbsp lime juice

1 tbsp vegetable or peanut oil

2 shallots, finely chopped

1 garlic clove, finely chopped

2 fresh green chilies, seeded and
    finely sliced

1 tsp black mustard seeds

1 tsp coriander seeds

5 tbsp grated palm sugar or
    brown sugar

5 tbsp white wine vinegar

1 tsp salt

pinch of ground ginger

Mango Chutney

Curry served with rice and chutney is a classic combinatiion, and Mango Chutney is always a favorite. This recipe is for fresh chutney, in which the mango is cooked for only a short time. The advantages are that it doesn't make a vast quantity or need to be left to mature, but nevertheless can be kept for a week.

• Put the mango in a non-metallic bowl with the lime juice and reserve.

• Heat the oil in a large skillet or pan over medium-high heat. Add the shallots and cook for 3 minutes. Add the garlic and chilies and cook for an additional 2 minutes, or until the shallots are soft but not brown. Add the mustard and coriander seeds and then stir.

• Add the mango to the pan with the sugar, vinegar, salt, and ginger and stir. Reduce the heat to its lowest setting and simmer for 10 minutes until the liquid thickens and the mango becomes sticky.

• Remove from the heat and let cool completely. Transfer to an airtight container, cover, and chill for 3 days before using. Store in the refrigerator and use within 1 week.

MAKES ABOUT 8 OZ/225 G

1–2 fresh green chilies, seeded or
    not, to taste, and finely chopped
1 small fresh Thai chili, seeded or not,
    to taste, and finely chopped
1 tbsp white wine or apple cider
    vinegar
2 onions, finely chopped

2 tbsp fresh lemon juice
1 tbsp sugar
3 tbsp chopped fresh cilantro, mint,
    or parsley, or a combination
    of herbs
salt
chili flower, to garnish

Chili and Onion Chutney

For a chili and onion raita,
stir 1¼ cups plain yogurt
into the chutney mixture
and chill for at least 1 hour.
Stir before serving and
sprinkle with fresh herbs.

• Put the chilies in a small non-metallic bowl with the vinegar, stir, and then drain. Return the chilies to the bowl and stir in the onions, lemon juice, sugar, and herbs, then add salt to taste.

• Let stand at room temperature or cover and chill for 15 minutes. Garnish with the chili flower before serving.

Index